The Gift of Justice

A Journey of Restoration with Dignity

Dr. Philip William Calvert

Published by Shaped By Grace, LLC

shapedbygrace.org

giftofjustice.org

This 40-day devotional is part of the author's "Gift of..." series. The theme of God's gifts to His people is the thread that connects each book in the series. As such, selected scriptures and concepts are used in each book to develop a coherent and wholistic narrative of God's love and provision for us. In this way, the books are integrally intertwined.

The devotional for day 39 is an adaptation from the author's handbook of God stories titled, "Praying through Scripture: Prayer Guide for Evangelism and Missions." © Dr. Philip William Calvert. 2008-2021.

Watch the author's video devotionals at christforlife.life

Listen to the author's devotionals at grace911.com

Front cover image by Philip William Calvert

Front cover design by Nathaniel Calvert

Look for other titles in the author's "Gift of..." series, including: *The Gift of Courage* © and *The Gift of Unity.*©

To order additional copies directly from the author, please visit giftofjustice.org

Contents

Contents

Forward

In the past year, the concept of "justice" often referred to as "social justice" has been at the forefront of cultural and political conversations in the United States and throughout much of the world. What has struck me in reading and listening to those conversations, especially in the media and on social media, is that the concept of justice means different things to different people. For some it is a term that inspires compassion and for others it is a concept that inspires anger and even violence.

In his newest devotional, *The Gift of Justice,* Phil Calvert offers an invaluable scriptural perspective on justice. What does justice mean to God? He starts with what he calls a simple definition, "...right behavior that is equitable and fair for everyone." He then develops the concept more fully from scripture to offer what he calls a "comprehensive paradigm." For instance, he notes that a society's view of justice can be seen in the way it treats its most defenseless people. He develops a biblical concept of justice through 40 daily devotions that include a discussion of an aspect of justice, a scriptural passage relevant to that concept, a short prayer, and an opportunity for the reader to note reflections. I highly recommend this book to anyone seeking a fuller and biblically based understanding of justice.

~Tom Campbell

Dedication

Most of us know people who have suffered tremendous injustice at the hands of others. The humiliation and pain inflicted upon them is staggering, and sometimes beyond human comprehension. In so many ways it defies logic that some people could be so cruel and vindictive toward others. Despite incredible odds many of those who are subjected to unspeakable injustice have managed to not only overcome the abuse and oppression, but have thrived because of it!

It is to all those who have overcome great odds, and who have maintained their dignity, grace, and humanity, that I dedicate this book. Indeed, human society would be far more capable of flourishing if we followed the lead of those who fully appreciate and understand the value of true justice, for through these people we see moments of restoration with dignity between offender and offended, perpetrator and victim.

Posthumously to Mr. Nelson Mandela, one of my heroes of modern statecraft, and to all those who have both pursued and set the gold standard of genuine justice, as well as those that desperately seek restorative justice in a very angry, broken, fallen, and hurting world, I dedicate this book. They are shining examples of the gift of justice. May the Lord greatly use their genuine example for His glory.

~Philip William Calvert

Acknowledgments

Great endeavors are team efforts requiring concerted energy. That is true in most areas of life, and it is certainly true with this book. Many hours of writing, editing, and manuscript preparation were involved in bringing this project to a successful completion. It was truly a labor of love by so many, and I thank them.

I especially want to thank my wife, Kristen, and our four children, Nathaniel, Benjamin, Rebekah Praise, and Abigail. They have been my never-ending source of encouragement and joy. The older I get, the more precious they become. Over the course of raising children, I have come to the full realization that, in many ways, my real legacy will be my own children. Of all the things I have been blessed with doing and seeing, by far my greatest accomplishment is raising children who love God, respect others, and work hard.

I want to say a special thank you to Cecilia Montijo for her expertise, help, and patience in guiding the formatting and mechanics of submitting this manuscript for publication. As always, she is a tremendous blessing indeed.

I also want to thank the wonderful people of Trinity Baptist Church for their love and affection. I am blessed to be called their undershepherd.

Introduction

The year was 1995. It was an otherwise nondescript year, though it stands out in my mind for two significant reasons. First, I was a recently married graduate student living in Reykjavík, Iceland. I was there as a Fulbright Scholar pursuing my doctorate in Political Science with concentrations in American Government, Comparative Politics, and International Relations. Though living near the Arctic Circle, I gravitated to news from around the world, which leads to the second indelible memory of that year. In the midst of my dissertation research and our European adventures, I was closely following the reports about something rather fascinating and inspiring occurring at the other end of the globe. The indomitable dissident, Nelson Mandela, who had spent some 27 years in prison for his opposition to the injustices of apartheid, was helping to establish a path toward national and racial reconciliation. This was a daunting task, as apartheid had been used as a lever of systemic and systematic racism and oppression in South Africa for 300 years. Having been granted his freedom in 1990 by President F. W. de Klerk, it was becoming increasingly obvious that Mr. Mandela was no ordinary statesman. He was attempting, and would achieve, something stunningly amazing. He set out, with the help of many other visionaries, to peacefully bring South Africa into the community of modern nations. It was a huge task. Nelson Mandela was up to the challenge.

Introduction

I watched from the vantage point of an island nation in the North Atlantic to see what would become of the valiant effort to peacefully transition South African society from one of overt racial discrimination to one of economic, political, and social inclusiveness. The future, indeed the soul, of the nation was at stake. In one of the best examples of seeking justice through restoration with dignity the world has ever seen, the Truth and Reconciliation Commission (TRC) was envisioned, created, and implemented. The TRC was established in 1995 with the explicit goal of leading South Africa through an intentional process of information gathering and dialogue that would result in a clearer understanding of the many injustices committed by numerous individuals and groups between 1960 and 1994. It was a process fraught with tremendous challenges, hurdles, and obstacles. Nonetheless, those intrepid justice warriors persevered and rose to the occasion. Many human rights violations were uncovered, and victims and perpetrators alike contributed their own stories to the overall narrative of the tragic events that had regrettably transpired. As evidence of the incredible change that was already taking place, Nelson Mandela had been elected President of South Africa in 1994. He served in that capacity until 1999. The TRC, despite its imperfections, had the desired effect in that South Africa peacefully transitioned from being a country divided by apartheid to becoming a representative democratic nation.

Introduction

It was a concerted effort that showed the world that a people could emerge from widespread oppression with their heart and soul intact. The work of the TRC, and Nelson Mandela's wisdom in pursuing a path of restoration with dignity, made a lasting impression on me as a political scientist, missionary, pastor, professor, husband, and father. The TRC remains the gold standard of national and interpersonal conflict resolution and restoration in the midst of unspeakable violations of the dignity and rights of our fellow human beings. Today there is still oppression in the world, whether it be economic, political, racial, or social injustice. The following devotionals are written to help remind us that justice is a human imperative, and that true justice is seen in restraint far more often than in retribution. Restraint is natural and organic. Retribution is contrived and forced, thereby leading to further victimization and revenge. Justice is not the advantage of the stronger, as famously stated by Thrasymachus in Plato's *Republic*. The Word of God conclusively shows that justice ultimately is in the Lord's hands, which is where it rightly belongs. When we love others as we love ourselves, we discover that justice is a gift from God, and that we can achieve it if we pursue it His way. This 40-day devotional is written to help each of us journey through the bitter betrayal, disappointment, and pain of injustice. Do not repay evil with evil. Rather, may you find healing and restoration with dignity.

Day 1

Don't be Deceived

A thread that weaves its way through scripture from Genesis to Revelation is the sad story of deception. From the fall of man through Adam and Eve, to the final persecution of the people of God, and from the forbidden fruit at the very beginning, to the final straw at the end of it all, the Bible clearly shows that when we take our eyes off our Heavenly Father, we are prone to being deceived and going astray.

Deception takes many forms, and comes in many shapes and sizes. One way we are deceived, indeed when we deceive ourselves, is when we allow our quest for justice, which is honorable and noble, to inflict undue pain and suffering on the object of our "righteous" indignation.

There is a specific reason this book's subtitle is, "A Journey of Restoration with Dignity." True justice is not the advantage of the stronger. The ends rarely justify the means.

No matter how serious the wrong, when we unmercifully seek revenge against those who have hurt us, we become no better than they are...and in most cases we become far worse. Friend, don't be deceived into thinking that the injustice you experienced warrants the abuse of another human being.

In so many ways, deception is a choice. When we choose to be wise in our own eyes, we are far more apt to being led away and led astray.

How do we avoid the road to destruction and stay on the path of righteousness? First, don't mock God. He remains on His throne. Second, understand that what you sow in the flesh you will reap in the flesh. Third, when you walk in the Spirit you will live by the Spirit. Fourth, never grow weary of doing good. Fifth, be kind and merciful to everyone, and don't be afraid to go out of your way to show an extra measure of grace to fellow believers, even those who have hurt you. Finally, don't be deceived. The sin of Satan is real, but so is the holiness of God. Friend, don't be deceived! Seek restoration with dignity even for those who have hurt you.

"Don't be deceived: God is not mocked. For whatever a man sows he will also reap, because the one who sows to his flesh will reap corruption from the flesh, but the one who sows to the Spirit will reap eternal life from the Spirit. So we must not get tired of doing good, for we will reap at the proper time if we don't give up. Therefore, as we have opportunity, we must work for the good of all, especially for those who belong to the household of faith."
Galatians 6:7–10

Prayer

Lord, give me spiritual eyes to seek justice without inflicting harm on others, even those who have wronged me. Though my pain is real, help me to see that subjecting those in the wrong to the same misery I endured is simply not justified, for I am not omniscient like You. In place of my wrath, give me a heart of compassion and mercy. Give me the wisdom to seek the kind of justice that honors You. Heavenly Father, help me to not be deceived into thinking that my role is to play Your part in this difficult situation. The journey to right a thousand wrongs begins with a heart of grace and mercy. Amen.

Reflection

_____

_____

_____

_____

_____

_____

_____

Day 2

Stand Up

A very simple definition of justice is right behavior that is equitable and fair for everyone. It is most often grounded in ethics, law, and religious beliefs. In this regard, every culture has a concept of justice because people generally have an innate sense of right and wrong. When someone unfairly violates a community norm or law, we naturally feel the injustice. This is why parents don't have to teach their children the feeling of injustice. That kind of indignation comes with living!

It is vitally important to come to the aid of those who are being wronged. To help us clearly understand the importance of standing up for others, let's begin with the fact that the Lord God Almighty loves you. In fact, He loves you enough that He sent His Son to die a cruel and humiliating death on a despised and heartless cross so that, while you were yet a sinner, you would be saved for an eternity with Him in Heaven. That was a huge sacrifice indeed!

What's more, until you heard the Good News of Jesus Christ you likely did not fully realize just how lost in your wicked ways you really were. By His grace and mercy, He stood up for you and saved you.

God likewise calls His people to stand in the gap for those who are downtrodden and oppressed. We are to be a voice for those who otherwise have no voice. It's not always easy, but defending the weakest and most vulnerable among us is part of our awesome and holy calling as children of God.

The world, as evident in how it treats the unborn and elderly, has no qualms about abusing its position of power and strength. To the world, might makes right and justice is defined by those with the ability to wield power. This is why a society losing sight of true justice will first see the ramifications in the way it treats the most defenseless people.

Those of us who truly know Christ as Lord and Savior have a genuine responsibility to help those in need, even if they are utterly abandoned and rejected by everyone else.

However, standing up never gives us a license to abuse our authority. As children of God our desire should be to see all people, even those who have perpetrated a crime against another person, restored to a right relationship with Him!

With merciful justice in mind, we should endeavor to speak for someone who has no voice. Stand up for someone today!

"Speak up for those who have no voice, for the justice of all who are dispossessed. Speak up, judge righteously, and defend the cause of the oppressed and needy."
Proverbs 31:8-9

Prayer

Lord, I want to stand up, and speak up, for those who have no voice, and for those too weak to stand on their own against powerful forces. Help me to do more than merely desire justice. Inspire me, dear Jesus, to fight for it. Give me the spiritual wisdom to uphold Your standard of grace and mercy so that, in my zeal for justice, I don't find myself fighting against You. Amen.

Reflection

_____

_____

_____

_____

_____

_____

_____

Day 3

Kingdom Heirs

Are you facing an unjust situation? Are you feeling dehumanized and devalued? If you are a child of God, you are an heir to the Kingdom of God! Before you lash out at injustice, it is healthy to be reminded of exactly who you are, to whom you belong, and to where you are ultimately going.

The word "purple" appears 48 times in the King James Bible. Purple represents royalty and majesty. It conveys the meaning of wealth and prosperity. Purple was the most expensive dye known to the ancient Israelites. During the Roman Empire, it took about four million mollusks to produce one pound of purple dye. To mock Jesus, His Roman tormentors put a purple robe on Him. Little did they realize that Jesus is truly the Messiah. They were quite literally abusing God the Son!

Just as Jesus was mocked, we will be ridiculed. We are heirs to the Kingdom, and we are heirs to His suffering at the hands of unjust men. But, fear not. Though as a Christian you may be on the wrong side of history, you are most certainly on the right side of eternity! We are joint heirs with Him in the Kingdom of God. You may not wear expensive purple clothing physically, but as a follower of Jesus Christ and Kingdom heir you are clothed in purple spiritually...and you look marvelous!

"The soldiers also twisted together a crown of thorns, put it on His head, and threw a purple robe around Him. And they repeatedly came up to Him and said, 'Hail, King of the Jews!' and were slapping His face. Pilate went outside again and said to them, 'Look, I'm bringing Him outside to you to let you know I find no grounds for charging Him.' Then Jesus came out wearing the crown of thorns and the purple robe. Pilate said to them, 'Here is the man!'"
John 19:2–5

Prayer

Thank You, Lord, for reminding me that I belong to You. Though I am being treated as a nobody, in Your eyes I am somebody. You loved me so much that You sent Your Son to die an unjust death for me. Before I rage against the injustice I feel, help me to appreciate the injustice Jesus suffered for me. I pray for those who are acting unjustly toward me. Amen.

Reflection

_____
_____
_____
_____
_____
_____
_____

Day 4

The Way of Justice

The Lord God Almighty is the Rock of our faith. He is unmovable. He is unchangeable. He is omnipotent. All that He does is perfect, good, true, right, and holy. He is faithful in all His ways. As the Creator of everything He is without prejudice toward anything. He has no reason to be passively aggressive with shameful bias. He has no motive to harbor unspoken hatred. He has no need for hidden agendas and secret schemes. What can we learn from God our Rock? We will never be a people of justice if we conduct ourselves in mischievous ways and with a scheming heart. Justice is most visible when it is transparent.

We can sound impressively egalitarian when speaking and posting publicly. We can be as "woke" as possible when we're around others. But you will never truly be a person of justice if you surreptitiously seek your own advantage over others, if you inwardly despise your neighbor, and if you manipulate the foreigner, stranger, and least significant among you. Justice is far more than a cliché. Justice is far more than a catchphrase. Justice is a way of life. True justice is a comprehensive paradigm. Do you really want justice for yourself? Live a life of righteousness toward others. Do you want justice for the weak? Act with integrity in all your dealings with the powerful.

Justice is not insisting that others cave to our demands or bend to our will. Justice is not a way to enrich ourselves. Not at all. Being a person of justice means possessing the quality of fairness with reasonable balance in all of our decisions and actions. How do we live like that? We learn to lean on the Rock of our faith! He is the true way of justice.

"The Rock—His work is perfect; all His ways are entirely just. A faithful God, without prejudice, He is righteous and true." Deuteronomy 32:4

Prayer

Dear Lord, I desire to influence others in the way of true justice. Help me to do more than merely speak about justice. Guide my heart so that my actions reflect my words. I desire to influence others in the way of righteous justice. Amen.

Reflection

_____

_____

_____

_____

_____

_____

Day 5

A Righteous Justice

To be a person of justice means that you are fair and reasonable. It is imperative to be balanced and measured in our behavior toward others. This is even more important when we are seeking justice. When a harm has been committed against you or others, your ability to righteously pursue justice will have a tremendous impact on the outcome.

Sadly, quite frequently we see justice pursued in such a way that grievous harm comes to everyone in the process. The great expenditure of people, time, and treasure does not deliver the result people want. In fact, the price that was paid may be simply too high. This does not mean that we should forego the pursuit of justice. We are called to be people of justice, and so we must strive to achieve it. The challenge, though, is to pursue it so that true justice is achieved.

How do you do that? It is far less about resources expended abundantly than it is about resources expended righteously! That is, pursue justice the right way.

When everything is said and done, the Lord cares far less about *what* you sacrificed pursuing justice and far more about *how* you pursued justice!

"Doing what is righteous and just is more acceptable to the LORD than sacrifice."
Proverbs 21:3

Prayer

Lord, help me to realize that if I expended everything I own in order to get justice my way it would not necessarily please You. Pursuing justice unjustly, despite the sacrifices I make in the process, would not garner Your approval. In fact, it would be unacceptable to You! Remind me today to seek justice and righteousness so that the result is pleasing to You. I want to glorify and honor You far more than I want to get my own way. Guide my path so that I pursue justice in the right way today. Amen.

Reflection

_____

_____

_____

_____

_____

_____

_____

Day 6

A Living Hope

As you approach the one-week mark in this 40-day devotional, this is a great opportunity to pause and consider the hope that you have in the midst of the injustice around you specifically, and in the world generally.

There is a great deal of injustice, whether it be economic, environmental, political, racial, or social. There is plenty of injustice to go around. The supply of injustice seems endless indeed. No matter how bleak and dark the circumstances are for you or someone you know, there is hope. Things are not as bad as they appear and they are better than they seem. In Christ there is new hope in the Lord's eternal justice!

In and through all of the injustice that you or your loved ones have experienced, there is yet hope. Hope is alive! In fact, while hopelessness leads to death, and death is itself hopeless, with new life there is always hope. Life itself is hopeful!

Hope gives us a vibrant energy and quest for life's beautiful blessings and great adventures because He is gloriously merciful. We have a living hope through Jesus Christ. Our inheritance is imperishable. Thus, let us live a life of truth and justice for Him.

A Living Hope

"Praise the God and Father of our Lord Jesus Christ. According to His great mercy, He has given us a new birth into a living hope through the resurrection of Jesus Christ from the dead and into an inheritance that is imperishable, uncorrupted, and unfading, kept in heaven for you." 1 Peter 1:3–4

Prayer

Lord, thank You for Your many mercies. help me to see the living hope that I have in You. Despite the injustice in the world around me, I want to truly experience the living hope that is only found in You. Give me the spiritual eyes to see that I have hope, and give me the grace to share that hope with those who are hurting in our unjust, unsettling, and upset world. Amen.

Reflection

_____

_____

_____

_____

_____

_____

_____

Day 7

Planted at Water's Edge

Where are you planted? Are your roots planted in the world or firmly near the Lord? Everyone is from somewhere and everyone is going somewhere. While we cannot change where we started from and where we have already been, we do have a great deal of control over where we are going.

Despite what you may have been told by people who do not have your best interest in their heart, you have a lot of influence over your future. In spite of the difficult circumstances that you face, and the injustice to which you have been subjected, you can chart a path for a brighter future. How do you do that? The next step in your journey of life and faith begins with where you are currently standing. Where are you right now spiritually? Where do you stand today with your faith in the Lord? How is your relationship with Christ? If you want the next step in your life to be a good one, you must start on good ground. You need to be planted at water's edge, where the soil is full of life and the spiritual water is abundant.

Are you planted at water's edge? If so, you will discover that enduring justice is found where the soil is full of the nutrients of righteousness and is watered with God's wisdom.

God's Word tells us that a man finds joy by delighting in the Lord's instruction. When we are planted at water's edge and live a life of righteousness according to the Lord's holy standard, we are nourished and we prosper in the work of our hearts and hands. Isn't that what you desire? Friend, you or someone you love may have experienced tremendous injustice, but that is not a reason to walk the path of sinners. No, not at all. In fact, joy is not found in the world. It is found in the Lord...it is attained by being planted at water's edge.

"How happy is the man who does not follow the advice of the wicked or take the path of sinners or join a group of mockers! Instead, his delight is in the LORD's instruction, and he meditates on it day and night. He is like a tree planted beside streams of water that bears its fruit in season and whose leaf does not wither. Whatever he does prospers. The wicked are not like this; instead, they are like chaff that the wind blows away. Therefore the wicked will not survive the judgment, and sinners will not be in the community of the righteous. For the LORD watches over the way of the righteous, but the way of the wicked leads to ruin."
Psalm 1:1-6

Prayer

Dear Jesus, help me to overcome the injustice and pain of my past. I acknowledge before You that I cannot change what has happened to me, where I have been, and what I have done. By Your grace I do have influence over my future. Through Your love for me I can chart a better course. Help me to steer clear of those who want to harm me or others. Set me firmly at water's edge, nourished by Your righteousness and watered by Your wisdom, so that every decision I make and every step I take will be a step of faith for Your glory. Help me to search for wholeness in You, and not in other people, things, or even in myself. You, Lord, are the answer to my deepest questions of significance. No amount of injustice can rob me of true joy in You when I am planted at water's edge. Amen.

Reflection

_____

_____

_____

_____

_____

_____

_____

Day 8

Beauty Among Thorns

There is a great deal of anger, animosity, anxiety, conflict, depression, hurt, misery, and violence in the world.

It seems that for every positive and touching news story there are ten horrible and tragic stories. Every day it appears that things are getting worse for mankind, and that injustice is the new norm. The world simply loves to dispense discouragement and misery. Indeed, there is a great deal of injustice, especially against the weak and powerless. Even a casual observer can see that the powerful are preying on the vulnerable in ways that even a few years ago would have seemed unimaginable.

It is in this context that we look at our own life and see that we are not immune to injustice and suffering. We walk on egg shells at work, at home, while driving, and even at the store! We look over our shoulders for danger as much as we look ahead for opportunity.

No matter what you're going through, even if you're a flower of peace among cacti of hate, there is beauty to be discovered and enjoyed for the eternal glory of God. Look for the good. Look for the joy. Look for the love. It is there. God's creation abounds in goodness.

In our troubled times, be the beauty and not the prickly! By the grace of God, you can be the beauty among thorns. You can choose to be an agent of injustice or a force for justice. It won't be by your power, for that is easily corrupted. In fact, don't purse justice in your strength. Ultimately you will not be content with the results. Let the Lord guide your steps. And, while you're walking with Him, look for the good all around you. Can you see the beauty in the midst of the thorns of life?

The Apostle Paul had a thorn in his flesh, but still he pressed on. If anyone had a good reason to complain about injustice it certainly was him! He was persecuted mightily, yet he honored the Lord gloriously! His life brought forth beauty in the midst of the spiritually hideous things of this world. His very life exemplified beauty among thorns!

"For if I want to boast, I will not be a fool, because I will be telling the truth. But I will spare you, so that no one can credit me with something beyond what he sees in me or hears from me, especially because of the extraordinary revelations. Therefore, so that I would not exalt myself, a thorn in the flesh was given to me, a messenger of Satan to torment me so I would not exalt myself. Concerning this, I pleaded with the Lord three times to take it away from me.

But He said to me, 'My grace is sufficient for you, for power is perfected in weakness.' Therefore, I will most gladly boast all the more about my weaknesses, so that Christ's power may reside in me. So I take pleasure in weaknesses, insults, catastrophes, persecutions, and in pressures, because of Christ. For when I am weak, then I am strong." 2 Corinthians 12:6–10

Prayer

Dear Lord, help me to find the beauty in all things. Even in the midst of the painful thorns in my life, I desire with all my heart to rest in You. Help me to boast about my weakness, loss, and pain, and not in my achievements, strength, and victories. I know that when I am weak in the eyes of man, I can be strong in the arms of Jesus. Help me to find the beauty among the thorns, and to bring glory to You in favorable and unfavorable circumstances. Amen.

Reflection

_____

_____

_____

_____

_____

_____

Day 9

Mountaintop or Hill to Climb

Are you facing a challenge today? Does your daily life feel like it is one long march on a dry, dusty trail up a steep hill? As you see those inevitable rises on the horizon, those potential trouble spots or serious challenges, is your first reaction to avoid them and try to go around them? Is your instinct to run at the first sight of the laborious hills we sometimes face? If so, perhaps by avoiding the hill to climb you are also missing the view from the mountaintop!

By fleeing from the hard work of the climb we often miss out on the beautiful view from the top of the mountain! Sometimes by avoiding the hike up the hill we miss out on a closer relationship with God. So, is that challenge you're facing a beautiful mountaintop or just another hill to climb?

The Lord is our salvation, so face the steep rise on your horizon with great resolve. The best way to overcome the injustice you have experienced is to go and live well. Let He Who indwells you be manifest in you and through you today! Whatever you are facing, have faith over fear because death is defeated and those in Christ are already victorious! Turn that hill to climb into a glorious mountaintop experience!

"I lift my eyes toward the mountains. Where will my help come from? My help comes from the L<small>ORD</small>, the Maker of heaven and earth. He will not allow your foot to slip; your Protector will not slumber. Indeed, the Protector of Israel does not slumber or sleep. The L<small>ORD</small> protects you; the L<small>ORD</small> is a shelter right by your side. The sun will not strike you by day or the moon by night. The L<small>ORD</small> will protect you from all harm; He will protect your life. The L<small>ORD</small> will protect your coming and going both now and forever."
Psalm 121:1-8

Prayer

Lord, help me to not get distraught when I face a steep hill to climb. Rather, grant me the grace to overcome the seemingly insurmountable obstacles of life with the joy of my salvation. I acknowledge that You are my helper in times of danger. You are my salvation. I love You, Lord. Amen.

Reflection

_____

_____

_____

_____

_____

_____

Day 10

A Ray of Hope

The world can be extremely discouraging. In fact, the world can by utterly cruel and unjust. It's as if the motto of the world is, "Get all you can get before someone else does. While you're at it, keep them from getting it too!" It is truly sad.

What the Kingdom of God offers is far better. There is always a ray of hope in the Lord. When we set our eyes on Jesus, and lean into His holiness and love, something amazing happens! We experience the joy of our salvation. Why? No matter how bleak things in the world seem to be, in Christ there is always a ray of hope! By looking to God in all things He can renew your faith in yourself and in mankind. A beautiful sunrise in the morning is a gift from God because the dawn brings with it hope for a better day. As the sun rises, even on the cloudiest of days, there is great expectation that God can, and will, do something spectacular in our life. For this reason, hope defeats injustice. Hope is victorious!

God is full of grace. He alone renews each day and infuses every morning with new hope. As such, we can wait on Him to intercede in our life at just the right time and in just the right way. Do you need Jesus today? Recall His faithful love and be refreshed. Let Him be your portion. Seek Him in all things.

"Yet I call this to mind, and therefore I have hope: Because of the Lord's faithful love we do not perish, for His mercies never end. They are new every morning; great is Your faithfulness! I say: The Lord is my portion, therefore I will put my hope in Him. The Lord is good to those who wait for Him, to the person who seeks Him."
Lamentations 3:21-25

Prayer

Dear Heavenly Father, in the midst of the challenges of my life I desperately need the hope that only comes from You. You are faithful. You are merciful. You are good. I place my faith, hope, and trust in You. Thank You for forgiving my sins, thank You for saving my soul, and thank You for giving me hope in all things. You, Lord, are my eternal portion! Because of that truth I can have joy even in the midst of injustice. Amen.

Reflection

_____

_____

_____

_____

_____

_____

Day 11

Let the Lord Avenge

It is fairly easy to find the evil in the world around us. Corruption, deceit, greed, hate, and hurtful words seem to be in ample supply. Despite all of the harm that has come our way, we must not take matters into our own hands by settling the score. There may be people right now who are persecuting you. Perhaps they are gossiping on social media, driving away your friends, insulting you, or otherwise causing you a great deal of distress and heartache.

There is no doubt that in these difficult moments of anguish it is hard not to respond with overwhelming force to those who have treated you unjustly. In your flesh you want revenge. Perhaps there are days when what you think about more than anything else is getting even.

The reality is that revenge is wrong. Sure, the thought of repaying evil with evil may cross your mind as you ponder the pain and trauma they have put you through, but playing the payback game is costly.

We must remember that vengeance belongs to the Lord. The task of settling accounts is up to Him. He, alone, can judge with complete knowledge and holiness. That is a really important truth.

So, what do you do with the painful injustices you have experienced? What do you do with the pain?

First, there are clear standards of conduct that, when violated, must be reported to the appropriate authorities. Of that there is no doubt. In some ways, that is the easy part.

Second, even after reporting the other person's behavior, we are called to bless them. We must pray for them and not curse them. That is not easy.

In fact, genuinely blessing your enemies will prove to be one of the most difficult things you can do in your Christian walk. Nonetheless, you can do it. In fact, you are called to do it.

"Bless those who persecute you; bless and do not curse. Rejoice with those who rejoice; weep with those who weep. Be in agreement with one another. Do not be proud; instead, associate with the humble. Do not be wise in your own estimation. Do not repay anyone evil for evil. Try to do what is honorable in everyone's eyes. If possible, on your part, live at peace with everyone. Friends, do not avenge yourselves; instead, leave room for His wrath. For it is written: Vengeance belongs to Me; I will repay, says the Lord." Romans 12:14–19

Prayer

Lord, help me to bless those who persecute me. It is difficult not to respond in kind to those who have treated me unjustly. In my flesh I want revenge. Some days, what I think about more than anything else is getting even and settling the score. I know it's wrong to want to repay their evil deeds with my own brand of justice. I can think of a few ways I could make them pay dearly for their actions. Yet, I know that is not what You have called me to do. You have called me to something far greater. Help me to respond according to Your righteous standard. Walk with me, Lord. Teach me Your ways. Let me rest in the fact that vengeance belongs to You. Amen.

Reflection

Day 12

Fruit of the Spirit

Responding to the injustice of the world with our own view of justice would, in so many ways, make life a little less complicated. When you are hurt, you hurt them back with equal or greater force, which is both a deterrent and a way to make you feel better about being wronged in the first place.

When you are insulted, you return the favor with a louder megaphone. When you are shamed, you take the fight to the court of social media. Pretty straightforward. However, for all those who claim to be followers of Jesus Christ, responding to injustice does not, and cannot, work that way. Our way is a more challenging way. Our path is a more difficult path. We are called to take the high ground.

While on the surface that does make our response to injustice more nuanced, at the core of our response is a simple concept. What is it? It is the fruit of the Spirit.

Because we claim to live by the Spirit, the Lord calls us, and expects us, to follow the Spirit. What is the significance of that statement? It means that we are to exhibit, at all times and in all things, the character of God. That is a tremendous, but glorious, expectation!

Our behavior must reflect the fruit of the Spirit, including being loving when we are hated, and being gentle when we are mistreated. We are to be filled with joy even in difficult circumstances. We are to be at peace, and live at peace, even when there is a battle for our emotions raging within us, and when there is a battle against the forces of injustice all around us. We are to be patient even when we are hurried and want something done our way, right here, and right now.

We are to show the goodness of the Gospel at all times so that fellow believers will be encouraged and those who don't know Jesus as Lord and Savior will be drawn to the heart of Christ.

We are to exhibit faith in all things, kindness toward all people, and we are expected to be in control of our desires, emotions, and all that we pursue.

The great news about possessing the fruit of the Spirit in these difficult times is that there is not a single law against living in such a way. You can freely live a life of fruitfulness.

Now is a great time to desire the fruit of the Spirit! Reach for the fruit of the Kingdom of God, not the junk food of the world. It will bring joy to your heart and peace to your home! May the fruit of the Spirit produce lasting justice in our day.

"But the fruit of the Spirit is love, joy, peace, patience, kindness, goodness, faith, gentleness, self-control. Against such things there is no law. Now those who belong to Christ Jesus have crucified the flesh with its passions and desires. Since we live by the Spirit, we must also follow the Spirit." Galatians 5:22–25

Prayer

Most gracious Heavenly Father, the real desire of my heart is to consistently exhibit the fruit of the Spirit. I know that You want Your people to be the feet, hands, and heart of Jesus Christ in these troubled times. In order to live like that, You have given us exceedingly clear instructions that we are to demonstrate the fruit of the Spirit in our daily life. Help me to live by the Spirit and to follow the Spirit on a daily basis so that I can lead others in the path of genuine justice. Amen.

Reflection

Day 13

Abide in Him

It is far easier to follow Jesus when things are going our way. When all is well, and we are affirmed and respected, we can claim to be Christians with ease. Indeed, it costs us very little when we act like a suffering servant but are treated like a spiritual king.

However, when we are mistreated for being a Christian it is far more difficult to remain faithful. It can sting really hard to sincerely serve others yet get treated like someone's servant.

Even worse is being maligned and persecuted for our faith. When we are betrayed, treated unjustly, and rejected it can be a challenge to find the heart, motivation, and strength to abide in Christ with the heart of Christ while serving others. In other words, it is easy to serve others when it pays handsomely, but really difficult to serve others when it costs us dearly.

Nonetheless, Jesus calls us to abide in Him. As we remain in Him, we get to enjoy a deeply personal and intimate relationship with our Lord and Savior. When we do that, we bear much fruit for God's Kingdom. Abiding in Him also means experiencing injustice like He did and, yet, staying focused on our Kingdom mission.

For those who don't faithfully remain in Him, they are cut off and thrown into the fire. While this is not about losing one's salvation, it does separate true believers from imposters.

Authentic followers of Jesus Christ will bear fruit. To be sure, an easy way to spot a Christian is by their fruit! Let us, therefore, abide in Christ.

Even when you have been subjected to the pain of injustice, remain faithful to the Lord. Abide in Him.

"Remain in Me, and I in you. Just as a branch is unable to produce fruit by itself unless it remains on the vine, so neither can you unless you remain in Me. I am the vine; you are the branches. The one who remains in Me and I in him produces much fruit, because you can do nothing without Me. If anyone does not remain in Me, he is thrown aside like a branch and he withers. They gather them, throw them into the fire, and they are burned. If you remain in Me and My words remain in you, ask whatever you want and it will be done for you. My Father is glorified by this: that you produce much fruit and prove to be My disciples." John 15:4-8

Prayer

Dear Lord, help me to remain steadfast in You. I know that when I abide in You, I will bear much fruit for Your glory. That is one of the deepest desires of my heart. Despite the glaring injustice in the world, and the painful injustice that I have personally experienced, I desire to honor You with my very existence. Thank You for loving me, thank You for saving me, and thank You for walking with me through the valley of despair and injustice. I love You, Jesus, and I commit to abiding in You. Amen.

Reflection

_____

_____

_____

_____

_____

_____

_____

Day 14

You Are Not Alone

Our God is a warrior! That's right. The God who loves you and who saved you is a warrior!

And, not only that, our God is among us. He is not the Lord Almighty who is distant and ambivalent to your suffering. He cares, He is there for you, and He can fight the fiercest battles on your behalf!

No matter what happens in your life, as a child of God He is with you. The love of the world is a self-serving and loud love, exemplified by the saying, "What have you done for me lately?"

God's love brings calm and quiet. His love rings in peace. His love bring joy. His love is deep, personal, and profound.

God wants you to sense His presence in your life. No matter what you have done, and no matter what has been done to you, you are not alone!

Your God is a warrior for justice and He is with you! He is on your side in ways that the world cannot fathom. He is there for you because He created you. As a child of God, He will not leave you. He will not run from your battles. He is a warrior!

"Yahweh your God is among you, a warrior who saves. He will rejoice over you with gladness. He will bring you quietness with His love. He will delight in you with shouts of joy." Zephaniah 3:17

Prayer

Lord, thank You for reminding me that You are a warrior who is there for me. You walk with me and You save me from my adversaries. Though injustice threatens to swallow me whole, You are my warrior who is faithful and holy. Thank You for being there for me in my darkest hour to fight my fiercest battles. Thank You for standing for me and with me against the forces of injustice. Amen.

Reflection

_____

_____

_____

_____

_____

_____

_____

The Gift of Justice

Day 15

Tower of Strength

There are many ways to seek justice, but they generally fall in two categories: the right way and the wrong way. When we seek justice at all costs, we will inevitably harm others in ways that create more injustice. Justice cannot be sought at all costs, for we will ultimately pay too high a price. Rather, the means we use to pursue justice must be commensurate with the initial harm and the potential remedy, all the while keeping in view restoration with dignity. Just as you would not use a chainsaw to remove a small splinter, so too must our pursuit of justice provide true relief without causing more damage to us, to the offending party, and to our community.

The starting point for a measured approach to justice is to rely on the Lord as our tower of strength. Knowing you have a secure and strong tower helps to encourage you, to motivate you, and to embolden you.

The Bible shows us that God is our mighty tower of strength. God is your strong tower! Rely on Him today! The wicked go astray in their pursuit of justice because they are their own "strong tower." However, for those in Christ we can be confident and measured in our pursuit of justice because our faith is in God. God is our strong tower.

36

"The name of Yahweh is a strong tower; the righteous run to it and are protected. A rich man's wealth is his fortified city; in his imagination it is like a high wall. Before his downfall a man's heart is proud, but humility comes before honor." Proverbs 18:10–12

Prayer

Dear God, I desperately want justice but I know it is wrong to pursue it at all costs. When the price of justice is too high it will simply cause more harm than good, and I will become the unjust one. I want to be a force for justice. May my actions not merely appease my personal desire for revenge and my own definition of justice. Help me to rely on You as my tower of strength so that I help restore those who are broken with dignity. I want to see justice in the world. Lord, let it begin in my heart. Indeed, I know that if I want universal justice, it must start close to home. Amen.

Reflection

_____

_____

_____

_____

_____

_____

Day 16

Broken Trust

While there are far more serious injustices to which we can be subjected, broken trust is one of the most painful experiences a person can go through in the normal course of life. The pain is so real, and lingers so long, because broken trust usually comes by the hand of a close friend or family member. Broken trust is real, and it really hurts.

Just like broken fences take longer to rebuild because the rubble must first be removed, so broken trust is difficult to repair because the rubble of pain must be healed. While you do not have to be the perpetual victim of someone else's behavior, we are called to forgive them. Whether or not the relationship is restored, forgiveness is required.

The injustice of broken trust does not negate the Lord's instruction to forgive. We must forgive others as Christ forgave us. That is not easy, but it is necessary. How do we do that? We must understand that forgiveness is less an appeal to emotion and more an act of our will according to the righteous standard of God. We are called to forgive others because of who God is, not based on what the other person has done and not relative to how badly they hurt us. Forgive as you have been forgiven and your heart can begin to be healed.

"He was praying in a certain place, and when He finished, one of His disciples said to Him, 'Lord, teach us to pray, just as John also taught his disciples.' He said to them, 'Whenever you pray, say: Father, Your name be honored as holy. Your kingdom come. Give us each day our daily bread. And forgive us our sins, for we ourselves also forgive everyone in debt to us. And do not bring us into temptation.'" Luke 11:1-4

Prayer

Jesus, thank You for teaching me to pray with faith in Your provision and in Your divine providence. There are people in my life that have broken my trust in them. It hurts greatly. I am struggling to trust again, and You remind me that I can always trust You to love me and to provide for me. Thank You, Lord, for that beautiful and appreciated reminder. Amen.

Reflection

_____

_____

_____

_____

_____

_____

Day 17

Worry Less, Live More

A repercussion of having suffered a significant tragedy or act of injustice is that it makes us prone to worry that it could happen again. It's the same phenomenon that occurs when athletes are injured. Once they have been hurt, they are more likely to take the next potential injury far more seriously because the road to recovery is long and difficult. Believers are called to live by faith, which requires us to overcome anxiety so that we can continue to minister in the name of Jesus Christ. You can always find time to worry. You have less time to live to the fullest. Stop worrying about life and start living it. We glorify God by living the life we're given, not by worrying about it! Jesus gave us an important word about worrying.

"This is why I tell you: Don't worry about your life, what you will eat or what you will drink; or about your body, what you will wear. Isn't life more than food and the body more than clothing? Look at the birds of the sky: They don't sow or reap or gather into barns, yet your heavenly Father feeds them. Aren't you worth more than they? Can any of you add a single cubit to his height by worrying? And why do you worry about clothes? Learn how the wildflowers of the field grow: they don't labor or spin thread.

Yet I tell you that not even Solomon in all his splendor was adorned like one of these! If that's how God clothes the grass of the field, which is here today and thrown into the furnace tomorrow, won't He do much more for you— you of little faith? So don't worry, saying, 'What will we eat?' or 'What will we drink?' or 'What will we wear?' For the idolaters eagerly seek all these things, and your heavenly Father knows that you need them. But seek first the kingdom of God and His righteousness, and all these things will be provided for you. Therefore don't worry about tomorrow, because tomorrow will worry about itself. Each day has enough trouble of its own."
Matthew 6:25–34

Prayer

Lord, help me to worry less and live more. This is my simple prayer. Help me to trust You more each day. Amen.

Reflection

_____

_____

_____

_____

_____

_____

Day 18

Peace to You

After His resurrection, Jesus greeted His disciples with a word of peace. He wanted them to believe in Him. He did not want them to be troubled.

Peace to you.

Jesus grants us peace, not so we can hoard it or hide it, but so that we can do something with it!

Peace to you.

As Christians, when peace like a river attends our way, we will naturally allow that peace to flow through us and into the world around us.

Peace to you.

We are saved *from* something, which is separation from God, and we are saved *for* something, which is eternal life. Therefore, we are called to live with the confidence that comes from being saved, set apart, and sent for His glory.

Peace to you.

Perhaps you have experienced a great loss or injustice. Just as the Lord Jesus did not want the sorrow of His crucifixion to be the end of His disciples' ministry, so too Jesus desires us to carry on with the proclamation of the Gospel.

Peace to you.

Before His ascension, Jesus told His disciples that the message of repentance and forgiveness would be preached to all nations, and that they were His witnesses. We are called to that same awesome and glorious task despite the injustices we have experienced.

Peace to you.

Whatever you have experienced, sharing Jesus with others will help you truly sense and share the peace of the Lord. Isn't that what you want today? Peace to you.

"And as they were saying these things, He Himself stood among them. He said to them, 'Peace to you!' But they were startled and terrified and thought they were seeing a ghost. 'Why are you troubled?' He asked them. 'And why do doubts arise in your hearts? Look at My hands and My feet, that it is I Myself!

Touch Me and see, because a ghost does not have flesh and bones as you can see I have.' Having said this, He showed them His hands and feet. But while they still were amazed and unbelieving because of their joy, He asked them, 'Do you have anything here to eat?' So they gave Him a piece of a broiled fish, and He took it and ate in their presence." Luke 24:36–43

Prayer

Dear Jesus, I desperately need peace in my life. I want to rejoice in the victory of Your resurrection. Help me to see the way forward in the midst of injustice as I look for the hope that can only be found in eternal life through You. Please show me a new and glorious path of grace and joy. I want to spend the remainder of my days meditating on You and not on the pain of the past. I love You, Lord. Amen.

Reflection

_____

_____

_____

_____

_____

_____

_____

Day 19

Fear is a Liar

When a person suffers a vicious attack or a great injustice, one of the lingering side effects can be fear.

Fear grips us. Fear paralyzes us. Fear steals our joy and tends to hinder us from clear thinking and decisive action.

The great news today is that God walks with us. He does not want us to live in fear. In fact, God strengthens us with His own righteous right hand! To be sure, God does not want a coward for a follower. That is an awesome truth.

When God called us to be missionaries, we had to overcome the fear of the unknown as we moved our three young children to South America. Not only did the Lord protect us, we went on to have our fourth child on the mission field.

Despite all of the unknowns and difficulties, we kept going. We repeatedly saw that fear is a liar. Because of that, we saw God do great things in our ministry.

What fear do you have to overcome so that you can more clearly see the Lord move in your life today? Call fear what it is. Fear is a liar. Now, move forward with your life in Christ!

"Do not fear, for I am with you; do not be afraid, for I am your God. I will strengthen you; I will help you; I will hold on to you with My righteous right hand."
Isaiah 41:10

Prayer

Dear Lord, I acknowledge before You that I sometimes put my fear before my faith. I admit that I often find myself running from You instead of toward You because I fear the world's reaction to my witness and the response of people close to me to my Christian beliefs. However, today I am calling fear what it is, which is a dirty, rotten liar. I desire that You would be the primary focus of my heart. Help me to finally and fully realize that fear is indeed a liar. Help me to better appreciate the peace that is found only in You. Today I declare that fear is a liar. Amen.

Reflection

_____

_____

_____

_____

_____

_____

Day 20

Don't Sell Out!

Now that you have made it to day twenty, don't stop now! What is your testimony worth? What price would you put on your walk with Christ? Would you sell out for a small sum?

For just thirty pieces of silver Judas Iscariot betrayed Jesus. Think about that for a moment. This man, who had spent a tremendous amount of time with Jesus in glorious and life-changing circumstances, was willing to throw everything away for worldly riches. Judas sold out, and did so cheaply!

The chief priests were more than willing to buy Judas' betrayal in order to arrest Jesus. They wanted Jesus, and they were willing to pay Judas for it. Judas wanted silver, and he was willing to sell Jesus for it. Judas sold out, and did so cheaply!

Judas surrendered his silver and lost his way! At the end of that sordid tale, Judas lost the silver, his life, and his eternity with the Christ with whom he had spent so much time...even time in fruitful ministry! Judas sold out, and did so cheaply!

But, see how quickly the chief priests and elders turned on Judas even though he felt tremendous remorse and returned the money. Judas sold out, and did so cheaply!

The religious elite essentially said, "Your sin is not our problem." They were supposed to be spiritual leaders, yet they acted wickedly! Judas sold out, and did so cheaply!

What lessons can we learn from these thirty pieces of silver? 1. Remain faithful. 2. Don't pursue dishonest gain. 3. Don't seek profit over people. 4. Understand that all wicked men, no matter how educated and refined they are, and no matter how much they flatter or finance you, will ultimately turn on you. 5. You will eventually lose the silver that cheated its way into your pocket. 6. There are sins so horrible they are impossible to buy back. 7. Some sins will even take your life.

Friend, don't sell out. Don't fear the future so much that you sell your tomorrow to the highest bidder. Remain faithful to the Lord Jesus! Whatever you have gone through, and whatever you are going through, stay strong and don't sell out!

"Then Judas, His betrayer, seeing that He had been condemned, was full of remorse and returned the 30 pieces of silver to the chief priests and elders. 'I have sinned by betraying innocent blood,' he said. 'What's that to us?' they said. 'See to it yourself!' So he threw the silver into the sanctuary and departed. Then he went and hanged himself." Matthew 27:3–5

Prayer

Lord, help me to not sell out to the world. Help me to not lose heart, and help me to not get complacent or discouraged. Help me to stay strong for Your glory. I want to remain steadfast and not be so captivated by the allure of the world that I sell out. As for me and my house, we are following the Messiah. The world can have its silver. Give me the Savior! I love You, Jesus. Amen.

Reflection

_____

_____

_____

_____

_____

_____

Day 21

Rough Seas, Great Sailors

Calm seas don't make great sailors! It's an old saying that holds a lot of truth. It is difficult to be a really good sailor if you have never experienced a raging sea. Just as water covers about 70% of the Earth's surface, so too do the raging seas of life come more frequently than we would like. On some days it seems that we experience one storm after another! It is possible that 70% of our life is spent stepping into, going through, or coming out of challenges that range from small to major. Yet, the storms of life strengthen our faith and resolve. If you're going through a dark valley or a fierce storm you can see it as pure misery or you can choose to see the good that could come from it. Because of what you've been through you could be stronger and wiser when the next storm in your life brews on the horizon. Be faithful to the Lord and He will walk with you. Your testimony reflects those golden opportunities of tremendous spiritual growth! Set sail on faith today!

"Are they Hebrews? So am I. Are they Israelites? So am I. Are they the seed of Abraham? So am I. Are they servants of Christ? I'm talking like a madman—I'm a better one: with far more labors, many more imprisonments, far worse beatings, near death many times. Five times I received 39 lashes from Jews.

Three times I was beaten with rods by the Romans. Once I was stoned by my enemies. Three times I was shipwrecked. I have spent a night and a day in the open sea. On frequent journeys, I faced dangers from rivers, dangers from robbers, dangers from my own people, dangers from the Gentiles, dangers in the city, dangers in the open country, dangers on the sea, and dangers among false brothers; labor and hardship, many sleepless nights, hunger and thirst, often without food, cold, and lacking clothing. Not to mention other things, there is the daily pressure on me: my care for all the churches."
2 Corinthians 11:22-28

Prayer

Dear Jesus, thank You for allowing me to cross the rough seas of life. They make me stronger, tougher, and wiser. Thank You for preserving me and saving me. Amen.

Reflection

_____

_____

_____

_____

_____

_____

_____

Day 22

Let God be the Judge

This is one of those devotionals that we would prefer to skip or misinterpret. The reality is that all of us will be harmed, injured, insulted, and suffer injustice, both great and small, during the course of our life. There is no way to avoid such hurtful and unfortunate circumstances. By this point in your life, you have no doubt come to that understanding and have also become resolved to the fact that everyone has battles to endure, many of which we must face alone.

How we deal with the hardships is just as important as the hardships themselves. What is in view here is far more than the typical daily struggles of life. We're talking about the kind of injustice that is egregious and injurious. How do we respond to that kind of pain?

First, you need to get out of any ongoing abusive situation. Whether it be emotional, financial, physical, or sexual abuse, you are created in the image of God and are wonderfully made by your Creator. Get away from the abuse.

Second, if you believe that a crime has been committed, it is imperative to contact the appropriate authorities. They are skilled and trained in handling such matters.

Third, now that you are safe and the legal process has been engaged, there is a huge step of faith that must be taken. It is time to trust the Lord in this situation. He loves you and wants the best for you. He is faithful. Place the healing process in His hands by forgiving those who have hurt you. Let the Lord Almighty be God Almighty. Judgement belongs to Him. Of course, the civil and legal system will pass judgement in their realm of expertise and responsibility. However, from a spiritual perspective it is crucial that you give the pain to Him. Neither carry the burden of remorse nor anger with you. You must forgive. God will judge. If you can do that, you will be well on your way to healing and moving forward in your life. Don't allow the hurt and injustice to define who you once were, who you are now, and who you are going to be. God created you for a purpose, and it most certainly was not to be defined by the pain of the world. Remove yourself from the harmful situation. Forgive. Let God pass judgement on the perpetrator. Live your life for the glory of the Almighty!

"Yahweh, the God of gods speaks; He summons the earth from east to west. From Zion, the perfection of beauty, God appears in radiance. Our God is coming; He will not be silent! Devouring fire precedes Him, and a storm rages around Him. On high, He summons heaven and earth in order to judge His people.

'Gather My faithful ones to Me, those who made a covenant with Me by sacrifice.' The heavens proclaim His righteousness, for God is the Judge."
Psalm 50:1–6

Prayer

Lord, help me to remain faithful to You and to Your commandments. I truly want to walk according to Your righteous standard and not according to the way the world says I should respond to the injustice that I have suffered. Help me to forgive and to allow You to judge those who have caused my pain and my suffering. Guard my heart and mind, dear Jesus, so that I do not respond by hurting others and destroying my Christian testimony. May I glorify You in all that I do and with all that I say. Amen.

Reflection

_____

_____

_____

_____

_____

_____

_____

Day 23

Don't Let the Fire Make You a Liar

Commitment. That is a big word. It's a serious word. A great way to explain the difference between involvement and commitment is with the metaphor of a bacon and egg breakfast. To put that delicious meal on your table required the chicken to be partially involved. However, the pig was totally committed!

All too often people make commitments they do not keep. While some people make promises knowing they cannot keep them, most people resolve to do something fully intending to carry through with their plans. Nonetheless, circumstances change and reality often conflicts with the vow that was uttered. What's in view for today is the commitment a person makes to the Lord when they face a difficult situation.

There are many instances where someone will try to bargain with the Lord when they are facing a crisis. They will say something like, "If You save me, I will start going to church." This is referred as "foxhole religion." Faith that is faked in the foxhole is no faith at all. It is a false faith. A foxhole faith is not a salvific faith. Such a person has no intention to fulfill the vow. They simply want to be rescued.

When it comes to justice, keeping your word is parament. Once you have entered the slippery slope of deceit it is hard to change course. Sadly, breaking the bond of your word also breaks the bond of trust. Trust is very difficult to regain, yet it is part of the foundation of restoration with dignity.

People are more likely to give you a measure of trust as the relationship begins than they are to trust you again once their confidence in you has been lost.

Justice requires trust. Trust requires you to fulfill your commitments. Thus, being a person of your word is critical to helping to establish justice in and through your life.

Even in the midst of the challenges of life, keep your word. Fulfill the commitments you made at the start of the difficulties and the fires you're facing. After the Lord delivers you, follow through on your word.

Don't let life get in the way of remembering the Lord's blessings. Has He blessed you? Praise His name! What promises, vows, and commitments have you made? Fulfill them. Justice depends on your commitment to integrity.

Don't let the fire make you a liar.

"'Simon, Simon, look out! Satan has asked to sift you like wheat. But I have prayed for you that your faith may not fail. And you, when you have turned back, strengthen your brothers.' 'Lord,' he told Him, 'I'm ready to go with You both to prison and to death!' 'I tell you, Peter,' He said, 'the rooster will not crow today until you deny three times that you know Me!'"

Luke 22:31–34

Prayer

Lord, please help me to fulfill my commitments. I want my life to count for something, and I know that all of my experience, knowledge, and skills amount to very little if the people that You have put in my path can't count on me. Without trust, I acknowledge that I cannot be a force for justice. Help me to be trustworthy so that I can lead others for Your glory. Amen.

Reflection

_____

_____

_____

_____

_____

_____

Day 24

Broken But Not Forsaken

One of the many difficult lessons we learn in life is that, at some point, we will feel quite broken about something that we have done, that has occurred, or that we are going through.

That *thing* will cause us so much grief and misery that it will break us down to the point of despair, discouragement, heartache, and loneliness. The trauma can even lead to severe depression.

It's not easy to predict when it will happen, and avoiding life's calamities is nearly impossible. Afterall, the source of the pain can be a sudden event or a person that is very close to us.

It might be a chronic health issue that developed suddenly or over time. Perhaps it's a dire financial situation resulting from a poor decision or the cascading effect of many smaller events.

Whatever it is, it is extremely unsettling. It can make us feel anxious, crushed, and upset. It could utterly shatter our self-confidence. It might leave us with a sense of uncertainty and maybe a little bitter toward someone or even toward God.

How are you personally doing today? Be honest with yourself. Is there a relationship that has caused turmoil in your life? Do you sense that your life is drifting a bit, and perhaps you're in a fog of conflict or turmoil?

Though we may be broken, God's people are not forsaken. God can heal and restore you wherever you've been, whatever you've done, and whatever has been done to you. Though we are broken by our sin or the behavior of others, we can still rejoice in the Lord just like Moses and Paul.

Is there a spiritual discipline or some other area of your life that you have neglected? Perhaps your relationship with your spouse or your children is in tatters. Perhaps your relationship with the Lord is not what it should be or what you want it to be.

This is a great opportunity to remind yourself who you are in Christ. You might be hurting, but by the grace of God you can find healing and love in the Lord.

You might be broken, but by the grace of God you are not forsaken! Your life can still reveal Christ to a lost and hurting world! In fact, God fully expects you to faithfully follow Him in spite of the adversities of life.

"Now we have this treasure in clay jars, so that this extraordinary power may be from God and not from us. We are pressured in every way but not crushed; we are perplexed but not in despair; we are persecuted but not abandoned; we are struck down but not destroyed. We always carry the death of Jesus in our body, so that the life of Jesus may also be revealed in our body."
2 Corinthians 4:7–10

Prayer

Lord, while I may have felt indestructible when I was younger, I certainly do not feel that way now. Maybe it's part of growing older and wise, but I know that I can be vulnerable and weak. Remind me that I am not destroyed even when the world strikes me down. Thank You for not abandoning me. I praise You that I can glorify You in the midst of my agony. Help me to rest in the shadow of Your loving protection. Amen.

Reflection

_____

_____

_____

_____

_____

_____

Day 25

A Way Out

There are numerous ways to get the attention of other people. It is possible to be so annoying that others take notice. It is possible to be so angry that others take notice. It is possible to be so talented that others take notice. Of course, not all interest is the same. Some interest will cause problems, like when a thief takes notice of you and your possessions, or when you have become that day's object of "interest" on social media. Rarely does it work out in your favor to get your fame for a day by being the talk of the internet! While going "gray" is helpful when there is great danger lurking around the corner, it is human nature to notice other people. You could be walking in a darkened forest and if there is someone there, even just one person casting a slight shadow, your eyes will be drawn to them. To be sure, there are some forms of being noticed that result in great blessings, like when you meet the person you will marry. Their interest in you will bring tremendous joy. We notice people. It's what we do. There are countless ways for people to take an interest in you.

While the causes of someone taking an interest in you are varied, and the results of that interest are many, there is one aspect of interest that is fairly uniform across cultures and around the world. If you stand up to tyrants and to the world, you will get noticed.

Nonetheless, there are times when you need to stand up. When you do, you'll get noticed, not because that was your goal, but because it will happen. It just does. If you ever come to the point in life where you decide you would like to meet new people, there is a way that is almost certain to help you meet new people. How? Simply serve others in the name of Jesus Christ by proclaiming the holiness of God. The world will send all kinds of critics your way! You will meet many new people, and you will meet them quickly.

The Apostle Paul had a missionary's heart. He desired to preach even when it was dangerous. What did he get for his faithful followship of Christ? Persecution. Just like Jesus. Undaunted, he fearlessly pursued God's plan for his life. By the grace of God, Paul unashamedly exemplified the Great Commission. He was not content to settle for a life of leisure and obscurity while the lost perished. He knew that the Lord had called him to something great. He stood up. He wanted to swing for the fence for the Kingdom of God.

Despite the many challenges he faced throughout his incredible ministry, until the Lord decided to call Paul home, the Lord always provided a way out. Sometimes the way out was unconventional, but God watched out for Paul. Are you being persecuted or experiencing injustice? God can provide a way out. Turn to Him today!

"But Saul grew more capable and kept confounding the Jews who lived in Damascus by proving that this One is the Messiah. After many days had passed, the Jews conspired to kill him, but their plot became known to Saul. So they were watching the gates day and night intending to kill him, but his disciples took him by night and lowered him in a large basket through an opening in the wall." Acts 9:22-25.

Prayer

Lord, let my life reveal You to a lost world that is desperately seeking meaning and significance. Help me to show the way to salvation through Christ even if that means I will get noticed. And, if I am noticed, and if I face persecution, trials, and tribulations, help me to overcome each act of injustice to which I am subjected until You call me home. Amen.

Reflection

_____

_____

_____

_____

_____

_____

_____

Day 26

A Fresh Wind

There are times when we realize that what we are doing is simply no longer working. For whatever reason the old ways of doing things are no longer effective. Take this opportunity to carefully consider how you treat other people. How is that working out for you? Make a change for the good. Will you start something fresh today? Be renewed with a fresh wind in your life. Be a fresh wind of revival in another person's life!

"The LORD then said to Moses, 'Stretch out your hand over the land of Egypt and the locusts will come up over it and eat every plant in the land, everything that the hail left.' So Moses stretched out his staff over the land of Egypt, and the LORD sent an east wind over the land all that day and through the night. By morning the east wind had brought in the locusts. The locusts went up over the entire land of Egypt and settled on the whole territory of Egypt. Never before had there been such a large number of locusts, and there never will be again. They covered the surface of the whole land so that the land was black, and they consumed all the plants on the ground and all the fruit on the trees that the hail had left. Nothing green was left on the trees or the plants in the field throughout the land of Egypt.

**Pharaoh urgently sent for Moses and Aaron and said, 'I
have sinned against Yahweh your God and against you.
Please forgive my sin once more and make an appeal to
Yahweh your God, so that He will take this death away
from me.' Moses left Pharaoh's presence and appealed to
the LORD. Then the LORD changed the wind to a strong
west wind, and it carried off the locusts and blew them
into the Red Sea. Not a single locust was left in all the
territory of Egypt." Exodus 10:12-19**

Prayer

Lord, search my attitude, deeds, and words. Am I being an
agent of injustice? Am I causing other people problems? If I
am, dear Jesus, I admit that it is not working very well. Help
me to find a fresh wind of joy in my heart and a fresh wind of
love for others. Help me to bless someone today! Amen.

Reflection

_____

_____

_____

_____

_____

_____

_____

Day 27

Disappointment is Personal

Disappointment is the displeasure or sadness that arises when our dreams, hopes, and plans go unfulfilled. While there are far worse experiences than disappointment, it is nonetheless a difficult situation through which to journey. Since any number of circumstances and people can lead to unmet expectations, it is important to consider two aspects of disappointment over which we have some control. The first is the goal itself. If you are prone to being disappointed with people and with God, you might have an issue with expectations that are disconnected from reality. This realization does not mean becoming mediocre. Rather, it means setting goals that stretch you but that also help you show grace when those plans are unfulfilled. The second aspect of disappointment is finding a healthy response to it. There are countless ways to respond to disappointment, many of which are destructive. The key is to preserve the relationship even when people disappoint you. Since disappointment is highly personal our response should be equally personal, which is to pray! Even when, and especially when, the disappointment involves an injustice, we must check our response against the Lord's instruction. What does He say? He tells us to pray and rejoice! That is how we constructively turn disappointment into delight!

"Rejoice in the Lord always. I will say it again: Rejoice! Let your graciousness be known to everyone. The Lord is near. Don't worry about anything, but in everything, through prayer and petition with thanksgiving, let your requests be made known to God. And the peace of God, which surpasses every thought, will guard your hearts and minds in Christ Jesus."
Philippians 4:4-7

Prayer

Dear Lord, thank You for giving me a purpose and a passion. I am prone to being disappointed when my goals are unfulfilled. While I want to constantly strive for excellence, help me to not get too disappointed when people don't meet my expectations. When I am unhappy with something, give me the grace to focus on You. When I sense an injustice has occurred, please guide my heart to take the issue to You in prayer. Amen.

Reflection

_____

_____

_____

_____

_____

_____

The Gift of Justice

Day 28

Live by Faith

The world has a lot to say about the "good life." Though definitions vary from culture to culture, there are certain patterns of thinking about the "good life" that are discernable across cultures. One of those patterns is living with a meaningful purpose. It is essential to our well-being and personal growth that we spend the one life that each of us has been given by living it to the fullest in Christ. He is the way, the truth, and the life. Follow His purpose for your life.

Are you nursing some bitterness? Is that the deeper life Jesus has for you? Are you harboring anger? Is that the beautiful life Jesus has for you? Are you holding on to an injustice that was committed against you? Is that the life of purpose Jesus has for you? This is not to minimize the real anger and pain you feel from past events and harsh words that have been spoken to you or about you. The hurt is raw and real.

Yet, if you truly desire to look forward to the *future*, you must be able to look beyond the *past* and see what the Lord is doing in your life *today*.

Look beyond yesterday. Afterall, God is the God of tomorrow because He is the God of eternity.

Whether you have no children or many children, there is one life that God has placed squarely in your hands. Whether you have a few friends or many friends, there is one life that God has placed squarely in your hands. Whether you work alone or you lead thousands of people, there is one life that God has placed squarely in your hands. What life is that? It is *your* life! At the end of the day, the one life you will be held accountable for living is your own. You may be held accountable for how you led others, raised others, and treated others, but you will also give an account for the way you actually lived *your* life. Let that thought sink in for a moment. What will you do with God's plan for *your* life? The answer is truly quite simple. You are called to bring glory to Him with the one life that you have been given. You are to tell others about Jesus Christ. You are to share the Gospel. You are to trust in God the Father in the name of Jesus Christ in the power of the Holy Spirit. You are to fearlessly love others. Regardless of the hurt and injustice you have experienced, go and boldly share the reality and truth of Jesus Christ today. Live by faith!

"For through the law I have died to the law, so that I might live for God. I have been crucified with Christ and I no longer live, but Christ lives in me. The life I now live in the body, I live by faith in the Son of God, who loved me and gave Himself for me." Galatians 2:19–20

Prayer

Lord, help me to live each day with the full knowledge that You are the life! The world promotes hedonism and materialism as the way to a happy life. The world loves stories of people getting mad and then getting even when they face injustice. The world teaches us to take all that we can and to seize the day for our own needs and for our own glory. Such a life only leads to discontentment and heartache. That's not living. That's not real life. At least it's not a truly meaningful life. Help me to focus on You and on Your way. The injustice that I have suffered is real, and it really hurts. However, I choose this day to pursue life. I will pursue forgiveness and joy. I want to live the rest of my life with real meaning and purpose for Your glory. May others in my life see my genuine passion for You. Amen.

Reflection

_____

_____

_____

_____

_____

_____

_____

Day 29

Who will Provide?

The rat race is a metaphor for an endless or pointless pursuit of something that is elusive. Once on the never-ending treadmill of life we strive simply for the sake of striving. The pursuit becomes the purpose. You know you are in the rat race when you see a crowd rushing to buy something and, suddenly, you feel the burning desire to have the same thing. Once you have made the purchase, you realize you don't like it, need it, or want it. That is the rat race. We hunt for the sake of the hunt, not because we are truly hungry. Why do we get on that treadmill of futility? There are many reasons, some of which are compelling. Other reasons are personal. Still other reasons are prideful. The common denominator among all of our reasons for futile pursuits is that at some level we fear the future. We want to be comfortable, taken care of, provided for, and secure. So, we run and run and run. People work their entire lives, and strive until they are exhausted and worn out, simply for the hope that one day they will be able to retire and have what they need. Is there some life-sustaining "thing" that you currently lack? You may lack wants, but your true needs are being met. Even if you have sinned, God can forgive and provide. No matter what has happened to you, and no matter what you have done, turn to the Lord. Don't commit an injustice simply to have a desire, dream, or want met. God will provide!

"And He said to Adam, 'Because you listened to your wife's voice and ate from the tree about which I commanded you, 'Do not eat from it': The ground is cursed because of you. You will eat from it by means of painful labor all the days of your life. It will produce thorns and thistles for you, and you will eat the plants of the field. You will eat bread by the sweat of your brow until you return to the ground, since you were taken from it. For you are dust, and you will return to dust.' Adam named his wife Eve because she was the mother of all the living. The LORD God made clothing out of skins for Adam and his wife, and He clothed them."

Genesis 3:17-21

Prayer

Lord, You know my many challenges. Give me faith so that I can rely on You for all things. I trust that You will provide.

Reflection

Day 30

The Righteous Know

Is there something, or some information, that you understand to be absolutely true? Is there something that you simply know is a fact? Actually, there are many things that you know to be true just like you know the back of your own hand.

Take, for instance, the fact that one plus one equals two. You know that one of something plus one of the same thing always equals two of those things. You just know.

When you are counting money, you don't sit down and develop a mathematical proof for the equation that one dollar plus one dollar equals two dollars. You just know.

At a baseball game, each score adds one point on the scoreboard. You don't need to be reminded by the announcer after each runner scores that one plus a number equals that number plus one. You just know.

If you are pulled over for speeding, you don't need the officer to explain that by driving ten miles per hour in addition to the maximum allowable speed means that you were going ten miles over the speed limit. You can argue all you want, but it won't change the facts. You just know.

If you are hungry, you eat something. If you are thirsty, you drink something. You don't need a daily crash course in anatomy and biology to understand that food reduces hunger and water quenches thirst. You just know.

There are some things that we just know. We don't even think about them. We don't need to prove them to be true every day. That would be annoying. That would be a colossal waste of your valuable time. When it comes to God, there are things that we know to be true. We don't need to reinvent the wheel every day. We know there is only one God. We know man is fallen and sinful. We know that sin separates us from God. We know that Jesus is the only way to salvation, which is by His blood that was shed on the cross. We know that Christ was crucified, buried, and resurrected, and that He will return in the future. We know that all those who believe in Christ as Lord and Savior will be with Him in eternity. You just know.

We also know that God calls all His people to righteousness. He punishes sin. God's people must reject the sinful things of the world. Those in Christ are to live joyfully, knowing our eternal destiny is secure. The people of God know that the poor have rights too. We are to be lovers of justice. Whether you are on the receiving end or the power end of justice, if you belong to the Lord you are called to act justly. You just know.

"An evil man is caught by sin, but the righteous one sings and rejoices. The righteous person knows the rights of the poor, but the wicked one does not understand these concerns." Proverbs 29:6–7

Prayer

Lord, I know that You saved my soul. I know that You call me to live according to Your righteous standard. I know that there are countless injustices in the world. I know that You call me to forgive those who have hurt me, and to ask those I have hurt to forgive me. I know that I am not to be an agent of injustice. Rather, You call me to pursue justice, even for those without power and with no voice. Help me, Lord, to pursue justice. I know that when I pursue You with all of my heart I will sing and rejoice. I want that kind of life, Lord. Hold on to me as I seek to uphold Your righteous standard. Amen.

Reflection

_____

_____

_____

_____

_____

_____

The Gift of Justice

Day 31

Woe to the Unjust

What does the word *woe* mean to you? If you were to define that word to someone who had never heard it before, what would you say? How would you describe it? How has woe affected your life? What does it signify to you personally?

Technically speaking, woe means great sadness. It can also refer to being in great distress. To add to someone's woes means to pile more distress onto their despair. That is pretty powerful. That is tragic! Have you ever been overcome by a woeful situation? Have you experienced excessive misery and sorrow? If you have, you know that you don't take that season of your life lightly, and you don't want to repeat it. In fact, you'll probably do just about anything to avoid returning to the days of your woe. Sadly, many people are the cause of their own woes. Their actions, deeds, and words get them into such trouble that their lot in life becomes woeful indeed. Make every decision a good one because if you make enough bad decisions eventually all of your options will be bad. God has something much better just waiting for His people. He wants us not to live in woe, but to live in wonder! How do we do that? A first step is not being a hypocrite! Any good we achieve in *looking* like a Christian will be wiped away by the *reality* of our hypocrisy. Woe to the unjust.

Do you want to live each day with the joy of your salvation? Uphold justice and mercy in your daily life. It's pretty simple. Be faithful, or woe to you.

"Woe to you, scribes and Pharisees, hypocrites! You pay a tenth of mint, dill, and cumin, yet you have neglected the more important matters of the law—justice, mercy, and faith. These things should have been done without neglecting the others. Blind guides! You strain out a gnat, yet gulp down a camel!" Matthew 23:23–24

Prayer

Lord, I love You. I want You as my Savior *and* as my Lord. I know this means that I must live according to Your righteous standard. When I do, I will be a living testimony of faith, mercy, and justice. That is the life I desire. Amen.

Reflection

_____

_____

_____

_____

_____

_____

_____

Day 32

Turn the other Cheek

I am not sure if I like this devotional. I find the Bible verses to be rather challenging, and they don't seem to fit our culture today. I do love the prayer at the end. I'm just not sure I like the devotional that holds me accountable. Here, let me show you what I mean.

We live in a world that places a high value on winning. We don't like losers. In fact, we dislike losing so much that many years ago we started giving trophies to everyone who competed. We stopped keeping score. We stopped saying a certain team won. We stopped grading in a serious way. In some places, we stopped grading altogether. We don't like losing. We want to win and we want everyone to feel like a winner. When we are confronted with our sin, we reject both the idea of sin and the "accuser." When we are wronged, we want to get even. The internet is full of real videos of real people acting like they own the world and nothing should be allowed to confront them in ways that make them feel average. So, we retaliate. Yet, if Jesus taught us anything it was to not get even. God's justice is better than our justice. We need to truly forgive and rely on Him. Today, you probably need to turn the other cheek in some situation. Now you know why I don't really like this devotional. Do *you* like it?

"You have heard that it was said, An eye for an eye and a tooth for a tooth. But I tell you, don't resist an evildoer. On the contrary, if anyone slaps you on your right cheek, turn the other to him also. As for the one who wants to sue you and take away your shirt, let him have your coat as well. And if anyone forces you to go one mile, go with him two. Give to the one who asks you, and don't turn away from the one who wants to borrow from you."
Matthew 5:38–42

Prayer

Lord, it can feel really good to get even. Sometimes I feel that Your justice is too slow in coming. I get impatient. I take matters into my own hands and I show the other person that I'm in charge and that I'm the boss. When I get even, I am wrong. Help me to rejoice when I turn the other cheek. Amen.

Reflection

_____

_____

_____

_____

_____

_____

_____

Day 33

The Strength of Justice

Justice is not a moment in time. Justice is not overpowering our adversaries by flexing our muscles. Justice is not a fleeting feeling that all is well with the world because *we* got *our* way! No, not at all.

We are living in times that are unprecedented in so many ways. There are many voices and people clamoring for *their* version of justice.

The problem is that they usually insist on justice according to their rules and to their version of reality.

Yet, that is not the way justice works! True justice is built on the enduring precepts and principles of God. Why?

He is still on His throne. He goes with His people in and through everything. Therefore, be strong and courageous!

What a timely message, and one that was given by Moses to Joshua as the people of God prepared to enter the Promise Land. Moses knew that their path was not going to be easy, but the journey was necessary. Moses admonished them to be courageous, resilient, and strong.

In our day we may have to sift through the voices and find strength in the justice of the Lord. What this world does not need is people flexing their muscles to manipulate the outcome in their favor.

If the solution cannot last beyond the fleeting influence of those in power, then however high-minded it sounds the solution is built on temporary force that will fade away, leaving even more injustice in its wake.

What followers of Jesus Christ must do is find strength in the Lord, for His justice is both endearing and enduring.

When we build our lives on His justice, we will be blessed with the desires of a righteous heart and the possession of His precious promises!

Friend, that is the only way to live for the Almighty.

"Moses then summoned Joshua and said to him in the sight of all Israel, 'Be strong and courageous, for you will go with this people into the land the LORD swore to give to their fathers. You will enable them to take possession of it.'" Deuteronomy 31:7-8

Prayer

Dear Lord, help me to find my true strength in You each day and in every dispute. The world says that I can do anything if I set my heart and mind on it. I have tried doing just that. It works for a while, but it always leaves me running on empty and feeling hopeless. When I lean on my own understanding, I find myself creating in my part of the world a version of justice that always meets my needs, but rarely benefits others. I know that is not right, and I know there is more to justice than me getting my own way. Sometimes I find that I am not even happy when I get my way exactly as I wanted it. I've come to the realization that what I really want is justice that endures. Help me, Lord, to stand for justice in Your strength and not by my own wisdom. Amen.

Reflection

_____

_____

_____

_____

_____

_____

_____

Day 34

Justice is the Foundation

God is God and we are not. That is a statement of eternal truth. Sometimes, it's a necessary reminder as well. It is a great place to start today's devotional.

Buildings that are constructed to code have a foundation. A good foundation is firm and strong. It will stand the test of time, and the ravages of the elements. The foundation will typically outlast every other part of the building.

Consider the great monuments and temples of the ancient world. Even if the upper portion of the structures are gone, we know that they once stood, where they once stood, and many other details by studying their foundations.

The oldest pyramids date back to roughly 2,600 B.C. Egypt's Pyramid of Djoser was built during that era. It is still standing, which means that it has been in existence for about 4,600 years.

If the visible part of the pyramid has eroded 10% then its foundation will not be exposed for another 41,400 years! Only then would its foundation begin to deteriorate. Good foundations last a very, very long time indeed.

It is critical for followers of Jesus Christ to understand the nature of God's throne. What does God's Word say about the foundation of His throne? The Bible says that the foundation of the Lord's throne is righteousness and justice. What is always in view from atop His throne is His holiness, love, and truth. That is an awesome foundation indeed!

Are you a child of God? Do you want the Lord to guide you, protect you, stand with you, and uphold your cause? The foundation of all that He does is righteousness and justice. He is holy and He will act accordingly. Since that is the case for Him, it is important for us to follow along carefully.

How do you align with His standard? How are you doing living like Jesus? If you want all of the benefits of being a follower of Jesus Christ, you need to walk like Jesus Christ. The foundation of all you do must be righteousness and justice. Do you have some work to do? Maybe some fences to mend?

"Righteousness and justice are the foundation of Your throne; faithful love and truth go before You. Happy are the people who know the joyful shout; Yahweh, they walk in the light of Your presence. They rejoice in Your name all day long, and they are exalted by Your righteousness.

For You are their magnificent strength; by Your favor our horn is exalted. Surely our shield belongs to the LORD, our king to the Holy One of Israel."
Psalm 89:14-18

Prayer

Dear Jesus, help the reality of Your justice and righteousness sink deep into my heart. I don't want to simply say that I am Your follower, I want to act, feel, speak, and think like Your follower. It's not always easy. In fact, it's rarely easy. Living like Jesus is often difficult, especially when I want my way or things are challenging and stressful. Remind me that Your throne is established for eternity and its foundation is righteousness and justice. Lord, I really needed to hear that today. Amen.

Reflection

_____

_____

_____

_____

_____

_____

Day 35

Justice will be Served

We absolutely love it when justice is served. We especially like it when justice is served piping hot to all those who need a healthy helping of reality. The bigger the dose, the better. Let them have it, Lord, is our rallying cry. Except, of course, when the person in the wrong is us. Then we want mercy, and plenty of it. Give us a second helping of it if necessary. Just let us not have to pay for what we've done.

How do we rationalize those two very different views of mercy and justice? How can I live my life expecting sweet mercy for me and a swift kick in the teeth for you?

The answer is a bit complex but it can be boiled down to a simple idea. We judge others by their worst actions but we want others to judge us by our best intentions. We want the benefit of the doubt while at the same time doubting the motives of others. Unless, of course, we get our way. Then we assume their motives are noble, pure, and right! Why not? If they affirm us, they must be good and right!

Nonetheless, God's justice will be served. It will be served right. It will be served on time and in His time. And, we better believe that it will be well-done!

"I know that the LORD upholds the just cause of the poor, justice for the needy. Surely the righteous will praise Your name; the upright will live in Your presence."
Psalm 140:12-13

Prayer

Lord, I know that You uphold the just cause of the poor. I know that You ensure justice for the needy. I never want to stand in the way of Your justice. Help me, in fact, to promote biblical justice. I want to stand for You, even if that means I must stand against the world, or stand against my own self-interest. When I do, I know that I will be able to praise Your name today. Loving You is a prelude to how I will walk in Your presence forever. Amen.

Reflection

_____

_____

_____

_____

_____

_____

_____

The Gift of Justice

Day 36

Sticks and Stones

Sticks and stones may break our bones, but words can never hurt us. Really? It is difficult to *walk away* from an insult when someone criticizes us to our face. It is really difficult to *scroll away* from an insult when it is made on social media. Those insults truly do hurt our heart. The things said about us and to us can sting for a long time, if not for a lifetime. We must, however, not let those injurious words negatively affect our lives. We are called to overlook the insults that come our way throughout our life. How can we develop the spiritual discipline to overlook an offense? First, we must find our ultimate affirmation in the Lord. When we seek man's approval, we are setting ourselves up for heartache because man's applause is always temporary. The accolades of man are typically based on a central idea, which is what you have done for that person most recently. If it is good, you are accepted. If it is bad, you are rejected. It's really quite simple. Second, we must be satisfied with the words from our mouth and the work of our hands. If you are genuinely satisfied with your actions, it will be easier to overlook the insults. Third, listen to wise counsel. Finally, listen to God's Word. Let God guide you. When you do that, you will be able to forgive the injustices and insults to which you are being subjected.

"A man will be satisfied with good by the words of his mouth, and the work of a man's hands will reward him. A fool's way is right in his own eyes, but whoever listens to counsel is wise. A fool's displeasure is known at once, but whoever ignores an insult is sensible."
Proverbs 12:14–16

Prayer

Lord, help me to try earnestly, live sincerely, work hard, and find my ultimate satisfaction in You. I know that when I listen to wise counsel, especially Your Word, I am not derailed or deterred by the insults of men. Help me to stay focused on You, and to overlook the unjustified criticism in my life. May my heart always be inclined toward You, and not toward the world. Thank You, Jesus. Amen.

Reflection

_____
_____
_____
_____
_____
_____
_____

Day 37

Grace and Truth

God's Word tells us that Jesus is the way, the truth, and the life. No one enters Heaven without a personal relationship with Him. Most Christians have heard that message many times because John 14:6 is quoted quite often. We live in a day when just about every sin ever conceived in the heart and mind of man is on full display on the streets, on the internet, and on television.

In fact, if you watch anything with a screen, you are mere seconds away, at any moment, from seeing something that will completely wreck your testimony. There is a sin, however, that may be a little less easy to spot. It often hides and lurks for just the right opportunity to pounce on its victim. It is the sin of injustice. Whether it be economic, political, racial, or social, true injustice truly does occur.

The challenge for followers of Jesus Christ is to be aware that it exists, to recognize it when it occurs, and to deal with it appropriately. Injustice is best dealt with by introducing it to truth. We must be honest about unjust behavior and apply truth to the situation to determine a constructive remedy. Not only must the injustice be confronted with truth, but the truth must be applied with grace. Therein lies the challenge!

If you look at what passes for remedies for injustice today you will notice that much of it is completely devoid of grace. If we want restorative justice, we must apply grace and truth.

"The Word became flesh and took up residence among us. We observed His glory, the glory as the One and Only Son from the Father, full of grace and truth."
John 1:14

Prayer

Dear Jesus, I needed to be reminded of Your grace and truth. I acknowledge that I can be good at knowing what is true. I can spot a lie a mile away, but I need help applying truth with grace. Help me to look at my own relationships to see where I have fallen short in applying truth with grace. If I have hurt anyone, please allow me to make amends. Though I may have been right, acting without grace is wrong. Amen.

Reflection

_____

_____

_____

_____

_____

_____

_____

Day 38

Defend the Oppressed

God clearly expects His people to come to the aid of the oppressed. We simply must defend the defenseless. In order to do that, it is important to define oppression. Let's first look at what oppression is not. Oppression is not necessarily being poorer than others. We are not oppressed when we are held accountable for our actions. We are not oppressed simply because we don't get what we want. Oppression is far more serious and it is important to confront it immediately and definitively. Oppressing someone is subjecting them to harsh and authoritarian treatment. A lot of what legitimately can be defined as oppression is done by a governing entity and those acting on behalf of that entity, whether with or without its knowledge or approval. However, less formal groups of people and even individuals who wield any kind of power can oppress others. In this way, a mob of people that regularly and systematically threatens others on an ongoing basis is oppressive. What is in view here is not a one-time act of random street violence but an orchestrated and repeated abuse of power by virtue of sheer numbers and the ability to use overwhelming force. Groups that supposedly despise oppression quite easily become the oppressors when they systematically treat others harshly as they wield informal and illegitimate power in their local community.

Defend the Oppressed

God calls us to defend the oppressed. It is an affront to Him when people abuse their power and take advantage of those who are least able to defend themselves. Justice requires fair treatment and an extra measure of grace and mercy. We must help those who are being oppressed, whether by mobs, the government, or individuals. It is our duty to plead their cause.

"Learn to do what is good. Seek justice. Correct the oppressor. Defend the rights of the fatherless. Plead the widow's cause." Isaiah 1:17

Prayer

Lord, it can be a daunting challenge to defend others. The fact they are being oppressed is proof that aggressors have a power advantage. There are many reasons that I do not want to get involved. However, I know that You call me to the righteous task of defending the defenseless. Help me to do so. Amen.

Reflection

_____

_____

_____

_____

_____

_____

_____

Day 39

Harvest in the Midst of Injustice

We hosted many volunteer teams from the United States that would help us with evangelism in unreached areas of our province. One day we had two volunteers in our car plus a local believer. We drove along a winding dirt road on the side of a massive volcano to see if there were any settlements there. While we did not find any villages, we had a spectacular view of the lake in the volcano's crater. After admiring God's creation, we drove down the volcano in search of a town we heard about the day before.

After getting directions from many people along the maze of mountain roads, we finally found the quiet town. As we entered it, one of the team members prayed that we would find a man of peace. We parked the car in the town square and started walking. We had gone about ten steps when we saw a U.S. twenty-dollar bill on the ground. To say the least, that was a very rare occurrence in that country. To find money on the ground was very strange indeed. Since we did not know to whom it belonged, we decided to use the money locally. It was time for lunch, so we decided that buying something to eat would be an excellent way to keep the money in the community. After walking around the town for some time, we asked one of the locals if there was a place we could eat. She asked us if we wanted *good* food or *just* food.

We decided that *just* food would be good enough. She pointed in the direction of a red house. After thanking her, we entered the otherwise nondescript building, sat down, and ordered a plate of chicken foot soup. As we were eating, we noticed a man eating alone in the corner of the room. He told us that he was a Christian from the capital city and that he was passing through on business. We told him we were looking for someone to help start a Bible study in their home. He said there was a Christian lady who worked at a local school. After paying his tab, he left. Our paths crossed for just a few minutes, but the information he provided was a blessing with eternal impact! We ultimately found the school and spoke with the Christian lady that the kind gentleman had told us about. She said that her father was the first Christian in the town and there were other Christians living there too. She gave us directions to their home. After we finally found their home, and they heard we were missionaries, they ran to greet us. They had been praying for over twenty years that someone would teach them the Bible! They were persecuted in the past for being Christians. We wept as we sat on bags of grain in their mill and heard their remarkable stories. They told us how the local nonbelievers tried to stone them two decades earlier when they showed a movie about Jesus in the town square. They had pure hearts, and harbored no enmity toward their persecutors. In fact, they desired them to know Jesus!

They drove us around their town and introduced us to other Christians scattered throughout the rural mountainside. This was such a blessed day as we were able to find several people of peace in that small town. Since then, this group of believers helped start a church in their community. There really can be a harvest in the midst of injustice!

"Then He said to His disciples, 'The harvest is abundant, but the workers are few. Therefore, pray to the Lord of the harvest to send out workers into His harvest.'"
Matthew 9:37-38

Prayer

Dear God, help me to see where You are working. Even in the midst of injustice You draw people to salvation, and You call Your people to join You. Here I am, Lord, send me! Amen.

Reflection

_____

_____

_____

_____

_____

_____

_____

Day 40

The Lord Speaks

A lot has transpired over the course of reading this book. You might have taken some notes, shared your ideas with others, and wrestled with some of your own feelings and thoughts.

After everything has been said and done, let's conclude with a final instruction from the Lord. What does God have to say specifically about the very important topic of justice?

He says emphatically that we are to administer justice and righteousness. We are to rescue people from oppression. We must not take advantage of others, whether they are widows, orphans, or foreigners. We are not to shed innocent blood.

The only way to accomplish that very important mission is to turn our hearts completely away from the gravitational pull of the world system. We must not harbor false idols of worship— whether they be material or spiritual. It is hypocritical to demand justice in society when our personal lives are a wreck.

Justice and righteousness are inseparable. History shows that those who want to overthrow their oppressor always face the real possibility that they will become the next tyrant. God tells us to administer justice *and* righteousness. They go together. The Lord has spoken.

"This is what the LORD says: Administer justice and righteousness. Rescue the victim of robbery from the hand of his oppressor. Don't exploit or brutalize the foreigner, the fatherless, or the widow. Don't shed innocent blood in this place." Jeremiah 22:3

Prayer

Lord, thank You for speaking to me during these forty days. I trust that You will use this time I have spent with You to help me grow deeper in my faith, in my walk, and in the conviction that I am, indeed, called to stand up for the oppressed. Yet, You also call me to be a force for justice in the right way. It is a great affront to You to seek justice in unjust ways. Help me to apply Your truth with grace. That is what You desire. You have spoken. I have heard You. I want to follow You. Amen.

Reflection

The Lord Speaks

This concludes Day 40. You made it!

Perhaps you were reminded of a biblical truth you heard a long time ago. Perhaps you have learned something new.

Have you sincerely prayed daily? Have you followed Jesus faithfully? Have you seen the hand of God work mightily?

Has the Lord spoken to you? If so, praise Jesus! You know that when the Lord speaks, we are to listen! When the Lord speaks, we are to obey. When the Lord speaks, we are to respond.

In short, we are to trust and obey. Indeed, there is no other way.

I pray that you have been blessed in some small but tangible way by *The Gift of Justice.* May it have been a journey of restoration with dignity.

Share your personal stories in the Grace Community online at facebook.com/shapedbygrace.org.

About the Author

Dr. Philip W. Calvert is an ordained minister and was a U.S. Fulbright Scholar to Iceland from 1994 to 1995.

In 1996 he received his Ph.D. in Political Science from Southern Illinois University-Carbondale, where he was a Morris Doctoral Fellow.

Dr. Calvert and his wife, Kristen, were appointed to the International Mission Board in 2003. They served on the mission field in Ecuador and Peru.

During their ministry as missionaries, they served in various roles from church planting to being the Seminary Connector for Ecuador and Peru.

Dr. Calvert taught at Southeastern Baptist Theological Seminary as an adjunct faculty member, Southwestern Baptist Theological Seminary as an Assistant Professor of History at the College at Southwestern, Truett-McConnell University as the Associate Professor of Missions and Associate Director of the World Missions Center, and Gateway Seminary as an adjunct faculty member.

Dr. Calvert currently teaches at Arizona Christian University as an adjunct faculty member, and he is the Senior Pastor at Trinity Baptist Church.

Phil and Kristen have four children: Nathaniel, Benjamin, Rebekah Praise, and Abigail. The Calvert family's passion is discipling believers to become full participants in the Great Commission.

You can watch his encouraging devotionals and sermons on his YouTube Channel at christforlife.life.

You can listen to his devotionals at grace911.com, you can follow him on Twitter at sheeptweet.com, and you can read his blog, "The Grace Connection," at shapedbygrace.org.

Be sure to join the exciting Grace Community online at facebook.com/shapedbygrace.org.